· Amazing Facts Book ·

OF BIBLE PROMISES

FOREWORD BY
DOUG BATCHELOR

The Amazing Facts Book of Bible Promises
© Copyright 2016 by Amazing Facts
P.O. Box 1058
Roseville, CA 95490

Discover Amazing Facts at www.amazingfacts.org.
Find more informative, life-changing Christian books,
magazines, DVDs, and more at afbookstore.com.

Compiled and written by Laurie Lyon
Edited by Steven Winn
Cover by Haley Trimmer
Layout by Greg Solie • AltaGraph

ISBN: 978-1-58019-647-5

Foreword

In 2013, a Northern California husband and wife were out for a leisurely stroll with their dog when they spotted the end of a rusted can sticking out of the dirt on their property. Stopping to investigate, they found, to their astonishment, that the can contained dozens of solid gold coins from the 1800s. Searching further, they found more rusty cans filled with gold coins, all in nearly mint condition.

Known as the Saddle Ridge Hoard, it was valued at over $10 million and is one of the greatest treasure troves ever discovered in the United States. Amazingly, the treasure had sat there for years, undiscovered, right in their own backyard!

It makes you wonder how many of us today are overlooking the much greater treasure trove of genuine happiness, joy, and peace that can be found only through the Word of God and a trusting relationship with our Creator.

God yearns to guide and comfort you today, and this book is designed to help you quickly find His encouragement regarding your particular situations.

I pray that you will be blessed as you come to trust in the One who freely offers you His wisdom and His "exceedingly great and precious promises" (2 Peter 1:4) and who wants to enter into a saving relationship with you today. You can count on Him to provide all the encouragement, strength, and hope you need for all of life's journey.

The many ministries of Amazing Facts focus on turning people's attention to God's Word. If you enjoy this little promise book, you'll certainly appreciate the epic treasures of truth you can discover at our many Bible websites — see page 138 for a list. These websites offer hundreds of free online resources, including fascinating Bible studies, books, and videos. Additionally, most of our websites even allow you to respond with Bible questions and prayer requests.

We hope to see you there!

Pastor Doug Batchelor
President, Amazing Facts

~ TABLE OF CONTENTS ~

BIBLE PROMISES FOR
WHEN YOU NEED
Peace

So many circumstances in our world—even day-to-day events—can leave you feeling distressed and frazzled. Peace is one of the gifts of the Spirit of God, and sometimes it may seem to be one of the most elusive. But God wants to change that. He desires to enter your heart and mind and bring you lasting peace! Read and savor His promises to you ...

"You will keep him in perfect
peace, whose mind is stayed on
You, because he trusts in You."

~ Isaiah 26:3 ~

*Focusing daily on the Lord and trusting
Him to direct your life will allow
Him to create His peace in you.*

"Oh, that you had heeded My
commandments! Then your
peace would have been like a river."

~ Isaiah 48:18 ~

*Peace comes as a natural result of
obedience to the law of God.*

"And His name will be called Wonderful, Counselor, Mighty God, Everlasting Father, Prince of Peace."

~ Isaiah 9:6 ~

Always remember that Jesus is your Source of genuine peace!

"Then He arose and rebuked the wind, and said to the sea, 'Peace, be still!'"

~ Mark 4:39 ~

The same Lord who calmed the savage storm longs to do the same in your life.

"For He Himself is our peace, who
has made both one, and has broken
down the middle wall of separation."

~ Ephesians 2:14 ~

*God, the ultimate peacemaker, can reconcile
even those with "impossible" differences.*

"Peace I leave with you, My peace I
give to you; not as the world
gives do I give to you."

~ John 14:27 ~

*The superficial, short-lived "peace"
of this world comes when everything
seems to go your way, but it can't
hold a candle to the all-encompassing
peace of Christ that lasts for eternity!*

"These things I have spoken to you,
that in Me you may have peace.
In the world you will have
tribulation; but be of good cheer,
I have overcome the world."

~ John 16:33 ~

*By remaining in Jesus Christ, you can find
the peace that transcends any troubles
you may experience in this world.*

"Therefore, having been justified
by faith, we have peace with God
through our Lord Jesus Christ."

~ Romans 5:1 ~

*Through His sacrifice, Jesus has made it
possible for us to be reconciled to God,
to be at peace with Him, and that is the
most vital and lasting peace we can have.*

"In everything by prayer and supplication, with thanksgiving, let your requests be made known to God; and the peace of God, which surpasses all understanding, will guard your hearts and minds through Christ Jesus."

~ Philippians 4:6, 7 ~

Go to God with all your needs and He will provide you with a peace that is even beyond comprehension!

. . . .

The Lord of peace invites you to lay your burdens at His feet. Give Him your frantic schedule, family disputes, financial troubles, and anything else that disquiets your soul. Trust in the ultimate Peacemaker and allow Him to rule in your life today!

BIBLE PROMISES FOR
WHEN YOU NEED

Encouragement

It happens to us all at one time or another. Life comes crashing in, weighing us down with burdens and cares of all kinds. It's easy to give in to our emotions, but it isn't the healthiest response—or the most helpful. If you're feeling overwhelmed by life, read and absorb these promises from your heavenly Father, precious reminders of His deep, never-ending love and concern for you!

"Though I walk in the midst of trouble, You will revive me; You will stretch out Your hand against the wrath of my enemies, and Your right hand will save me."

~ Psalm 138:7 ~

Whatever troubles perplex you in this life, God is always close at hand, reaching out to deliver you.

"Be of good courage, and He shall strengthen your heart, all you who hope in the LORD."

~ Psalm 31:24 ~

In any situation, God will give you courage from above if you put your trust in Him.

**"The eternal God is your refuge, and
underneath are the everlasting arms;
He will thrust out the enemy from
before you, and will say, 'Destroy!'"**

~ Deuteronomy 33:27 ~

*There could be no better refuge than
the all-powerful God of the universe
whose strong but gentle arms will always
support and defend you without fail!*

**"He gives power to the weak,
and to those who have no might
He increases strength"**

~ Isaiah 40:29 ~

*Though this world often saps your strength,
God is an unwavering source of power.*

"Peace I leave with you, My peace I give to you; not as the world gives do I give to you. Let not your heart be troubled, neither let it be afraid."

~ John 14:27 ~

Jesus will provide His peace to enable you to rise above any challenge.

"Being confident of this very thing, that He who has begun a good work in you will complete it until the day of Jesus Christ."

~ Philippians 1:6 ~

It is God's intention to save you for eternity; He won't give up on you!

"Therefore humble yourselves under the mighty hand of God, that He may exalt you in due time, casting all your care upon Him, for He cares for you"

~ 1 Peter 5:6, 7 ~

Trust that God is guiding you and wants you to place all your worries into His capable hands.

"Let us run with endurance the race that is set before us, looking unto Jesus, the author and finisher of our faith"

~ Hebrews 12:1, 2 ~

Jesus, the Author of your faith, will give you all the stamina you need to carry you through.

"For I am persuaded that neither death nor life, nor angels nor principalities nor powers, nor things present nor things to come, nor height nor depth, nor any other created thing, shall be able to separate us from the love of God which is in Christ Jesus our Lord."

~ Romans 8:38, 39 ~

Nothing can separate you from His love—it's impossible!

. . . .

Be encouraged in the knowledge that God is with you always and His love for you is rock solid!

BIBLE PROMISES FOR
WHEN YOU NEED

His Grace

Every one of us has broken God's law. Whether you've strayed unintentionally or with rebellion in your heart, there is a path to forgiveness and reconciliation with the Lord. Read these assurances from His Word …

**"Surely He scorns the scornful,
but gives grace to the humble."**

~ Proverbs 3:34 ~

*It's a good starting point when
you recognize and admit that
you need God's help.*

**"But God demonstrates His own love
toward us, in that while we were
still sinners, Christ died for us."**

~ Romans 5:8 ~

*Even when you've turned away from
Him and gone your own way, Jesus has
immeasurable compassion toward you.*

"In Him we have redemption through
His blood, the forgiveness of sins,
according to the riches of His grace."

~ Ephesians 1:7 ~

*It is only through Jesus that we
can receive the grace of God.*

"For all have sinned and fall short
of the glory of God, being justified
freely by His grace through the
redemption that is in Christ Jesus,
whom God set forth as a propitiation
by His blood, through faith."

~ Romans 3:23–25 ~

*Jesus paid the ultimate price so
that, by trusting in Him, you can
be made right with God.*

"If we confess our sins, He is faithful
and just to forgive us our sins and to
cleanse us from all unrighteousness."

~ 1 John 1:9 ~

*If you admit your wrongdoing to
God and turn away from it, He
promises to wash it all away.*

"Therefore, having been justified by
faith, we have peace with God through
our Lord Jesus Christ, through whom
also we have access by faith into
this grace in which we stand, and
rejoice in hope of the glory of God."

~ Romans 5:1, 2 ~

*Because of what Christ has done, you
can have real hope for the future.*

"May our Lord Jesus Christ Himself, and our God and Father, who has loved us and given us everlasting consolation and good hope by grace, comfort your hearts and establish you in every good word and work."

~ 2 Thessalonians 2:16, 17 ~

Receiving God's grace propels you into doing good works.

"But we believe that through the grace of the Lord Jesus Christ we shall be saved"

~ Acts 15:11 ~

When you receive His forgiveness you are also receiving the gift of eternal life.

"Now all things are of God, who has reconciled us to Himself through Jesus Christ, and has given us the ministry of reconciliation."

~ 2 Corinthians 5:18 ~

After forgiving you, God asks you to share the good news of His grace with others.

"For sin shall not have dominion
over you, for you are not under
law but under grace."

~ Romans 6:14 ~

*When God forgives you, He also
empowers you to begin living a
victorious and obedient life for Him.*

. . . .

*Because Jesus Christ laid down His life for
you, the door of grace is always open. You
can go to your heavenly Father anytime and
receive the gifts of forgiveness, reconciliation,
and salvation.*

BIBLE PROMISES FOR
WHEN YOU'RE FEELING
Worthless

This world sometimes leaves us feeling kicked, empty, and wondering if it's all worth it—or if we are worth it. But God leaves no doubt of the tremendous value He places on every human life, including yours …

"So God created man in His own image; in the image of God He created him; male and female He created them."

~ Genesis 1:27 ~

Your value begins with the fact that you are made by the hand of the Creator in His very image.

"Can a woman forget her nursing child, and not have compassion on the son of her womb? Surely they may forget, yet I will not forget you."

~ Isaiah 49:15 ~

Even if you are forsaken by family and friends, you are always cherished in the heart of God.

"For I know the thoughts that I
think toward you, says the LORD,
thoughts of peace and not of evil,
to give you a future and a hope."

~ Jeremiah 29:11 ~

*God's thoughts toward you are wonderful,
and He has great plans for your life!*

"Yes, I have loved you with an
everlasting love; therefore with
lovingkindness I have drawn you."

~ Jeremiah 31:3 ~

*His love for you is relentless,
immeasurable, and infinite.*

"But God demonstrates His own love toward us, in that while we were still sinners, Christ died for us."

~ Romans 5:8 ~

Our Father in heaven loves you so intensely that He allowed His own Son to die in your place before you ever repented.

"Knowing that you were not redeemed with corruptible things, like silver or gold ... but with the precious blood of Christ."

~ 1 Peter 1:18, 19 ~

God was willing to pay the highest price in the universe to redeem you—the blood of His dear Son.

"Behold what manner of love the
Father has bestowed on us, that we
should be called children of God!"

~ 1 John 3:1 ~

*God actually considers you His
very own precious child.*

"Now then, we are ambassadors for Christ,
as though God were pleading through us"

~ 2 Corinthians 5:20 ~

*God has given you a high calling as an
ambassador to share His great love with others.*

"But God, who is rich in mercy, because of His great love with which He loved us, even when we were dead in trespasses, made us alive together with Christ ... that in the ages to come He might show the exceeding riches of His grace in His kindness toward us in Christ Jesus."

~ Ephesians 2:5, 7 ~

Your heavenly Father has planned a magnificent, never-ending future for you.

"Therefore, if anyone is in Christ, he is a new creation; old things have passed away; behold, all things have become new."

~ 2 Corinthians 5:17 ~

If you belong to Jesus, you have a brand new, sparkling-clean life in Him.

. . . .

You belong to God, and as long as you cling to Him, no one can take that from you. His Word overwhelmingly confirms that you are His cherished treasure!

BIBLE PROMISES FOR
WHEN YOU NEED
Strength

This world generates endless challenges, some of which can sap our strength and leave us feeling drained and helpless. But you never need to feel powerless. Cherish these verses from God's Word …

"He gives power to the weak, and to those who have no might He increases strength. Even the youths shall faint and be weary, and the young men shall utterly fall, but those who wait on the LORD shall renew their strength."

~ Isaiah 40:29–31 ~

God will strengthen you if you simply lean on Him.

"The LORD is my strength and song, and He has become my salvation; He is my God, and I will praise Him."

~ Exodus 15:2 ~

You can always turn to the Source and find new strength in Him.

"Be strong and of good courage,
do not fear nor be afraid of them;
for the LORD your God, He is the
One who goes with you. He will
not leave you nor forsake you."

~ Deuteronomy 31:6 ~

*With the Almighty God by your side,
you are stronger than an army.*

"I can do all things through
Christ who strengthens me."

~ Philippians 4:13 ~

*You can conquer any obstacle and overcome
any problem as long as you cling to Jesus.*

"I will strengthen you, yes, I will help you, I will uphold you with My righteous right hand."

~ Isaiah 41:10 ~

The highest Power in the entire universe promises to continuously help and strengthen you!

"Be strong in the Lord and in the power of His might. Put on the whole armor of God, that you may be able to stand against the wiles of the devil."

~ Ephesians 6:10, 11 ~

The Lord wants to empower you today with His armor of truth, righteousness, the gospel of peace, faith, salvation, the Word of God, and prayer.

"Be of good courage, and He shall strengthen your heart, all you who hope in the Lord."

~ Psalm 31:24 ~

If you keep on trusting the Lord, drawing courage from Him and His Word, He will provide all the fortitude you need.

"And He said to me, 'My grace is sufficient for you, for My strength is made perfect in weakness.' Therefore most gladly I will rather boast in my infirmities, that the power of Christ may rest upon me. ... For when I am weak, then I am strong."

~ 2 Corinthians 12:9, 10 ~

When you recognize your own weakness, God can come in and fill you with His perfect strength.

"The LORD is my rock and my fortress and my deliverer; my God, my strength, in whom I will trust; my shield and the horn of my salvation, my stronghold."

~ Psalm 18:2 ~

The Lord is your strength plus everything else that you need in every situation.

. . . .

Let the limitless power of God permeate your life today to encourage and strengthen you!

BIBLE PROMISES FOR WHEN YOU NEED

Wisdom

Whether you're in the midst of a major decision or simply want to make the best day-to-day choices, wisdom is a necessity. According to Scripture, you can go to God at any time and receive the gift of wisdom from above. And, unlike the wisdom of this world, God's wisdom won't let you down! Consider His promises ...

"The fear of the LORD is the beginning
of wisdom; a good understanding have
all those who do His commandments."

~ Psalm 111:10 ~

*Wisdom starts with utmost respect
for God and obedience to His
uplifting commandments.*

"If any of you lacks wisdom, let
him ask of God, who gives to all
liberally and without reproach,
and it will be given to him."

~ James 1:5 ~

*God has an unending supply of wisdom
and is more than willing to give you all
that you need today if you ask Him.*

"Behold, You desire truth in the inward parts, and in the hidden part You will make me to know wisdom."

~ Psalm 51:6 ~

If you are honestly seeking God's will for your life, He will reveal His wisdom in your heart and mind.

"That the God of our Lord Jesus Christ, the Father of glory, may give to you the spirit of wisdom and revelation in the knowledge of Him."

~ Ephesians 1:17 ~

One of the most important applications of wisdom is to enhance your relationship with Jesus and your knowledge of Him.

"He stores up sound wisdom for the upright; He is a shield to those who walk uprightly."

~ Proverbs 2:7 ~

If you are living a life of righteousness in Christ, you can depend on God to provide an abundance of wisdom and keep you on the right track.

"But of Him you are in Christ Jesus, who became for us wisdom from God—and righteousness and sanctification and redemption."

~ 1 Corinthians 1:30 ~

Did you know Jesus became wisdom for you, and everything else that you need for salvation? What a wealth of wisdom is available through studying the life of Christ, who was filled with all wisdom!

"But it will turn out for you as an occasion for testimony. Therefore settle it in your hearts not to meditate beforehand on what you will answer; for I will give you a mouth and wisdom which all your adversaries will not be able to contradict or resist."

~ Luke 21:13–15 ~

If you rely on Him, God promises to give you such great wisdom when you witness for Him that those who oppose the truth will be silenced.

"The wisdom that is from above is first pure, then peaceable, gentle, willing to yield, full of mercy and good fruits, without partiality and without hypocrisy."

~ James 3:17 ~

The wisdom of this world is based in selfish desires and yields bitter fruit, but God's wisdom consists of the purest attributes and yields the happiest results.

. . . .

The God of all wisdom invites you to come to Him today and learn from Him. He is more than willing to guide every step you take and keep you on the path of salvation!

BIBLE PROMISES FOR
WHEN YOU'RE FEELING

Angry

It's one of the most common of human emotions, and sometimes there's good reason for it. Yet if uncontrolled, anger can be very damaging to your mental and spiritual well-being and even your physical health. Thankfully, God's Word gives great guidance regarding this powerful emotion, whether you are on the giving or receiving end ...

"An angry man stirs up strife, and a furious man abounds in transgression."

~ Proverbs 29:22 ~

It's so easy to make a mistake when your heart is filled with rage, to do or say things you will later regret.

"'Be angry, and do not sin': do not let the sun go down on your wrath, nor give place to the devil."

~ Ephesians 4:26, 27 ~

Often, it takes time to cool down after your anger has peaked, but the Bible advises you to let go of your anger as soon as possible to keep from sinning.

"A fool vents all his feelings, but a wise man holds them back."

~ Proverbs 29:11 ~

Restraint will benefit you much more than unleashing your feelings of anger.

"A soft answer turns away wrath, but a harsh word stirs up anger."

~ Proverbs 15:1 ~

The next time someone comes at you with claws extended, try a gentle response.

"He who is slow to anger is better
than the mighty, and he who rules
his spirit than he who takes a city."

~ Proverbs 16:32 ~

*One of your most potent weapons against
anger is the attribute of patience.*

"The discretion of a man makes
him slow to anger, and his glory
is to overlook a transgression."

~ Proverbs 19:11 ~

*It takes wisdom and strength from above
to let the discourtesy and rudeness
of others pass without retaliation.*

"A gift in secret pacifies anger, and a
bribe behind the back, strong wrath."

~ Proverbs 21:14 ~

*If someone with whom you were angry gave
you a nice gift, might it soften your heart?*

"Let every man be swift to hear,
slow to speak, slow to wrath; for
the wrath of man does not produce
the righteousness of God."

~ James 1:19,20 ~

*Here is the best reason for a follower
of Christ to avoid anger.*

"Rest in the LORD, and wait patiently for Him; do not fret because of him who prospers in his way, because of the man who brings wicked schemes to pass. Cease from anger, and forsake wrath; do not fret—it only causes harm. For evildoers shall be cut off; but those who wait on the LORD, they shall inherit the earth."

~ Psalm 37:7–9 ~

Even anger because of the temporary prosperity of the ungodly can have a negative effect on God's people and should be avoided.

"But now you yourselves are
to put off all these: anger,
wrath, malice, blasphemy, filthy
language out of your mouth."

~ Colossians 3:8 ~

*Remember that every scriptural command
is also a promise: God promises to give
you the power to do what's right!*

. . . .

*God is ready and willing to help you conquer
this potentially explosive emotion and defeat
any unresolved anger in your life today!*

BIBLE PROMISES FOR
WHEN YOU ARE

Anxious

Worry and anxiety are all too common in our hurried, stressful, unpredictable lives. For some, anxiety is an infrequent occurrence; for others, it's a constant, distressing companion. Most of us fall somewhere in between. But God wants something better for us. You can claim these encouraging promises from your loving Father in heaven ...

"Be anxious for nothing, but in
everything by prayer and supplication,
with thanksgiving, let your requests
be made known to God; and the
peace of God, which surpasses all
understanding, will guard your hearts
and minds through Christ Jesus."

~ Philippians 4:6, 7 ~

*God invites you to come to Him with all your
concerns and needs; He longs to help you
find positive solutions to your problems.*

"Peace I leave with you, My peace I give to you; not as the world gives do I give to you. Let not your heart be troubled, neither let it be afraid."

~ John 14:27 ~

It's no ordinary peace Jesus offers you, but a powerful peace that works to eclipse your fear and anxiety.

"Trust in the LORD with all your heart, and lean not on your own understanding; in all your ways acknowledge Him, and He shall direct your paths."

~ Proverbs 3:5, 6 ~

If you're anxious over choices you must make, put your entire faith in the God of your life and He will steer you in the right direction.

"Cast your burden on the LORD, and He shall sustain you; He shall never permit the righteous to be moved."

~ Psalm 55:22 ~

God wants you to lean on Him for support; He will carry all your burdens and keep you from slipping.

"And let the peace of God rule in your hearts, to which also you were called in one body; and be thankful."

~ Colossians 3:15 ~

God will drive out your anxious thoughts and fill your heart and mind with peace when you focus on Him.

"I will both lie down in peace,
and sleep; for You alone, O LORD,
make me dwell in safety."

~ Psalm 4:8 ~

*A lack of proper rest only increases anxiety;
trust your problems to the Lord and go to
sleep knowing He is watching over you.*

"Fear not, for I am with you; be
not dismayed, for I am your God.
I will strengthen you, yes, I will
help you, I will uphold you with
My righteous right hand."

~ Isaiah 41:10 ~

*It's safe to release all your fears and
worries into God's capable hands,
knowing that He is right beside you,
holding you up and providing the help
and strength you need each day.*

"And my God shall supply all your need according to His riches in glory by Christ Jesus."

~ Philippians 4:19 ~

Worrying over material needs is a waste of energy; our all-powerful God owns the entire universe and will take care of you—His precious child!

. . . .

Grasp the solid reassurance in God's Word and know that He will stay right with you through any circumstances life can throw your way!

BIBLE PROMISES FOR
WHEN GOD SEEMS
Distant

Probably all of us have had days
when God seems especially
far away. Even the psalmist David
sometimes felt abandoned by God.
Yet he wouldn't turn away from the
Lord; instead, he would seek God
more intensely. His faith paid off,
and so will yours if you cling to God
regardless of your feelings. Absorb
these reassurances from His Word …

"And those who know Your name will put their trust in You; for You, LORD, have not forsaken those who seek You."

~ Psalm 9:10 ~

If you are honestly seeking God, you can be sure He hasn't disowned you!

"Draw near to God and He will draw near to you."

~ James 4:8 ~

If you come to Him, the Lord is ready and willing to draw you into a closer relationship.

"But from there you will seek the LORD your God, and you will find Him if you seek Him with all your heart and with all your soul."

~ Deuteronomy 4:29 ~

It takes willingness and effort on your part to seek God, but the Bible confirms that you will be greatly rewarded for that effort.

"For He Himself has said, 'I will never leave you nor forsake you.'"

~ Hebrews 13:5 ~

If you belong to Him, you will never be truly alone.

"The LORD of hosts is with us; the
God of Jacob is our refuge."

~ Psalm 46:7 ~

*The God of the entire universe stands
with you and will help you!*

"For the LORD will not cast
off His people, nor will He
forsake His inheritance."

~ Psalm 94:14 ~

*It is God's desire and intention to
save you; He's not in the business
of throwing people away.*

"The LORD is near to those who have a broken heart, and saves such as have a contrite spirit."

~ Psalm 34:18 ~

When you are at your weakest point, God is close by to help you.

"All that the Father gives Me will come to Me, and the one who comes to Me I will by no means cast out."

~ John 6:37 ~

If you have given your heart to Jesus, you can be sure He will never push you away.

"Behold, I stand at the door and knock.
If anyone hears My voice and opens
the door, I will come in to him and
dine with him, and he with Me."

~ Revelation 3:20 ~

*Jesus knocks at your heart's door;
have you invited Him in lately?*

**"I am with you always, even
to the end of the age."**

~ Matthew 28:20 ~

*If you are His follower, Christ's
straightforward promise to you is
that He will be with you and will see
you through every aspect of your life
until the very end of the world.*

. . . .

*Aren't you glad the Bible leaves
no doubt on this subject? If you're
seeking God, He is with you at all
times, even when your emotional
state makes it difficult to sense His
presence. You are His beloved child!*

BIBLE PROMISES FOR
WHEN YOU ARE
Scared

On this rapidly decaying planet where bad things happen 24/7, it's easy to get caught up in an unhealthy pattern of giving in to fearful thoughts. God doesn't want us to be controlled by fear. He desires that we conquer our fears by trusting in Him. Read His words ...

"I sought the LORD, and He heard me, and delivered me from all my fears."

~ Psalm 34:4 ~

If you seek His presence and His will, God will give you courage for whatever you face in life!

"But He said to them, 'Why are you fearful, O you of little faith?' Then He arose and rebuked the winds and the sea, and there was a great calm."

~ Matthew 8:26 ~

Jesus has the power to dispel your fears and bring a great calm to your life!

"Wait on the L ORD; be of good courage,
and He shall strengthen your heart."

~ Psalm 27:14 ~

*God is with you at all times and is
a constant Source of strength!*

"Do not be afraid of sudden terror,
nor of trouble from the wicked
when it comes; for the L ORD will
be your confidence, and will keep
your foot from being caught."

~ Proverbs 3:25, 26 ~

*Be assured that even in scary situations
God is right beside you to help you.*

"Peace I leave with you, My peace I give to you; not as the world gives do I give to you. Let not your heart be troubled, neither let it be afraid."

~ John 14:27 ~

If you let Him, Jesus will give you His peace that is more powerful than any fear.

"For God has not given us a spirit of fear, but of power and of love and of a sound mind."

~ 2 Timothy 1:7 ~

This is God's desire for all His children— hearts not controlled by fear but by His love and power, resulting in sensible, logical thoughts and cognitive clarity.

"God is our refuge and strength,
a very present help in trouble.
Therefore we will not fear, even
though the earth be removed."

~ Psalm 46:1, 2 ~

*Through tumultuous events, you can
put your faith in God; He will always be
with you and will be your security.*

"For you did not receive the spirit
of bondage again to fear, but you
received the Spirit of adoption by
whom we cry out, 'Abba, Father.'"

~ Romans 8:15 ~

*When you become a child of God,
He breaks those bonds of fear.*

"There is no fear in love; but perfect love casts out fear."

~ 1 John 4:18 ~

Let God fill your heart with His love, keep focusing on Him, and your fears will fade away.

"The LORD is the strength of my life; of whom shall I be afraid?"

~ Psalm 27:1 ~

With the most powerful Being in the universe as your defender, you really have no one to fear.

. . . .

Why not bring your fears to God right now? His Word confirms that He longs to help you manage any fear in your life today!

BIBLE PROMISES FOR WHEN
YOU ARE WORRIED ABOUT

the Future

Our largely unpredictable future and active imaginations often combine to cause us to fear what's ahead on the road of life. But your heavenly Father has the desire and power to chart a course for you that ultimately ends in joy. Read His promises ...

"For I know the thoughts that I think toward you, says the LORD, thoughts of peace and not of evil, to give you a future and a hope."

~ Jeremiah 29:11 ~

There's no doubt that God has wonderful things in mind for your future!

"These things I have spoken to you, that in Me you may have peace. In the world you will have tribulation; but be of good cheer, I have overcome the world."

~ John 16:33 ~

Although this world is full of troubles, Jesus assures you He has conquered it all and will help you do the same.

"A man's heart plans his way, but the LORD directs his steps."

~ Proverbs 16:9 ~

You can be sure you're moving in the right direction only when you seek God's help.

"Teach me good judgment and knowledge, for I believe Your commandments."

~ Psalm 119:66 ~

God's Word and His commandments hold critical keys to making good decisions for your future.

"The LORD also will be a refuge for the oppressed, a refuge in times of trouble."

~ Psalm 9:9 ~

Whatever rough spots you encounter on your path, you can always hide yourself in Him.

"And in the days of these kings the God of heaven will set up a kingdom which shall never be destroyed ... and it shall stand forever."

~ Daniel 2:44 ~

God's ultimate plan for your future is to save you in His eternal kingdom of love.

"For our citizenship is in heaven, from which we also eagerly wait for the Savior, the Lord Jesus Christ, who will transform our lowly body that it may be conformed to His glorious body."

~ Philippians 3:20, 21 ~

Jesus promises you a glorious future if you are faithful to Him.

"And God will wipe away every tear from their eyes; there shall be no more death, nor sorrow, nor crying. There shall be no more pain, for the former things have passed away."

~ Revelation 21:4 ~

God's deep desire is to give you a destiny overflowing with joy!

"You will guide me with Your counsel, and afterward receive me to glory."

~ Psalm 73:24 ~

God will show you the way, both in the present and into eternity, if you keep on trusting Him.

"I will instruct you and teach you in the way you should go; I will guide you with My eye."

~ Psalm 32:8 ~

God is the perfect GPS; if you depend on Him for guidance, you can't go wrong.

. . . .

God has promised to guide your steps and provide for your needs when you seek Him and His truth through His Word and trust in Him with all your heart. Will you choose to put Him first in your life today?

BIBLE PROMISES FOR
WHEN YOU ARE
Grieving

No one travels through life without, at some point, experiencing the loss of someone or something dear. The loss of a loved one through death is one of life's most intense challenges, and the pain can be overwhelming. But God doesn't leave you to suffer alone ...

"Surely He has borne our griefs and carried our sorrows; yet we esteemed Him stricken, smitten by God, and afflicted."

~ Isaiah 53:4 ~

Jesus, the greatest empathizer, understands what you are going through and will remain with you.

"Blessed are those who mourn, for they shall be comforted."

~ Matthew 5:4 ~

The Lord will wrap His arms of love and comfort around those who trust in Him.

**"He heals the brokenhearted
and binds up their wounds."**

~ Psalm 147:3 ~

*Lean on God and allow Him to continue
the process of healing your broken heart.*

**"Blessed be the God and Father of
our Lord Jesus Christ, the Father of
mercies and God of all comfort, who
comforts us in all our tribulation,
that we may be able to comfort
those who are in any trouble."**

~ 2 Corinthians 1:3, 4 ~

Comforting you is God's specialty.

"Fear not, for I am with you; be not dismayed, for I am your God. I will strengthen you, yes, I will help you, I will uphold you with My righteous right hand."

~ Isaiah 41:10 ~

God promises to be with you and get you through this time of intense disappointment and loneliness.

"Yea, though I walk through the valley of the shadow of death, I will fear no evil; for You are with me; Your rod and Your staff, they comfort me."

~ Psalm 23:4 ~

Depend on His guidance to lead you out of that dark valley.

"But I do not want you to be ignorant, brethren, concerning those who have fallen asleep, lest you sorrow as others who have no hope. For if we believe that Jesus died and rose again, even so God will bring with Him those who sleep in Jesus."

~ 1 Thessalonians 4:13, 14 ~

As believers, we have hope of the resurrection promised by God.

"And God will wipe away every tear from their eyes; there shall be no more death, nor sorrow, nor crying. There shall be no more pain, for the former things have passed away."

~ Revelation 21:4 ~

In the new earth that God has promised to create, He will dry your tears.

"For the trumpet will sound, and the dead will be raised incorruptible, and we shall be changed. ... So when this corruptible has put on incorruption, and this mortal has put on immortality, then shall be brought to pass the saying that is written: 'Death is swallowed up in victory.'"

~ 1 Corinthians 15:52, 54 ~

At Christ's return, those who belong to Him will be raised and given life that will never end.

. . . .

Cling to the Lord and He will comfort you through the process of grieving and, in the future, will replace your sorrow with great, unending joy!

BIBLE PROMISES FOR WHEN YOU ARE STRUGGLING

with Guilt

We all make mistakes, and God's Word says we all have sinned. No matter how you came to your situation or how long you've carried that distressing burden of guilt, God is ready with the solution. His arms are outstretched to you. Look at all He will do for you ...

"For God did not send His Son into the world to condemn the world, but that the world through Him might be saved."

~ John 3:17 ~

It's not God's purpose to condemn you; it's His desire to take away your sins and save you through Jesus Christ.

"For He made Him who knew no sin to be sin for us, that we might become the righteousness of God in Him."

~ 2 Corinthians 5:21 ~

Jesus not only died for your sins, He took your sins upon Himself so He could give you His righteousness— His right standing with God.

"In Him we have redemption through His blood, the forgiveness of sins, according to the riches of His grace."

~ Ephesians 1:7 ~

Through the sacrificial death of Christ, you are given forgiveness and salvation as a free gift.

"'Come now, and let us reason together,' says the LORD, 'Though your sins are like scarlet, they shall be as white as snow; though they are red like crimson, they shall be as wool.'"

~ Isaiah 1:18 ~

God invites you to talk it over with Him, and He promises an outcome of great relief for you!

"If we confess our sins, He is faithful and just to forgive us our sins and to cleanse us from all unrighteousness."

~ 1 John 1:9 ~

All you need to do is tell God where you went wrong, and He will take care of everything else and wash it all away.

"For I will be merciful to their unrighteousness, and their sins and their lawless deeds I will remember no more."

~ Hebrews 8:12 ~

In His great mercy, God erases your sin from His memory!

"As far as the east is from the west, so far has He removed our transgressions from us."

~ Psalm 103:12 ~

It gives you a wonderful feeling of freedom to be separated from your sins.

"There is therefore now no condemnation to those who are in Christ Jesus, who do not walk according to the flesh, but according to the Spirit."

~ Romans 8:1 ~

If you follow Jesus and stay true to Him, you don't have to worry about the judgment; your guilt is a thing of the past.

"Therefore, if anyone is in Christ, he is a new creation; old things have passed away; behold, all things have become new."

~ 2 Corinthians 5:17 ~

In addition to cleansing away all of your sins through the blood of the Lamb, God gives you a brand-new life!

. . . .

Why not go to God right now and accept His wonderful gift of forgiveness through Jesus Christ? You have nothing to lose and eternity to gain!

BIBLE PROMISES FOR
WHEN YOU'RE FEELING THE

Weight OF THE World

ON YOUR SHOULDERS

Life is tough, and the burdens it hands you can be so hard to bear. But you don't need to carry them alone ...

"Cast your burden on the LORD, and He shall sustain you; He shall never permit the righteous to be moved."

~ Psalm 55:22 ~

God is glad to carry your burdens and give you the daily strength you need.

"Is this not the fast that I have chosen: To loose the bonds of wickedness, to undo the heavy burdens, to let the oppressed go free, and that you break every yoke?"

~ Isaiah 58:6 ~

It's not God's will that you should be crushed down with excessive burdens; let Him free you today.

"Come to Me, all you who labor
and are heavy laden, and I will give
you rest. Take My yoke upon you
and learn from Me, for I am gentle
and lowly in heart, and you will find
rest for your souls. For My yoke is
easy and My burden is light."

~ Matthew 11:28–30 ~

*Jesus will remove your heavy
burden of guilt and hopelessness
and give you true rest in Him.*

"For I, the LORD your God, will hold your right hand, saying to you, 'Fear not, I will help you.'"

~ Isaiah 41:13 ~

God promises to support and help you through every trial.

"Therefore humble yourselves under the mighty hand of God, that He may exalt you in due time, casting all your care upon Him, for He cares for you."

~ 1 Peter 5:6, 7 ~

Just knowing your heavenly Father cares about you personally can make any load seem lighter.

"Even to your old age, I am He, and even to gray hairs I will carry you! I have made, and I will bear; even I will carry, and will deliver you."

~ Isaiah 46:4 ~

The Lord desires to constantly support you throughout your life, with the intention of saving you eternally.

"He will feed His flock like a shepherd; He will gather the lambs with His arm, and carry them in His bosom."

~ Isaiah 40:11 ~

The Good Shepherd will gladly bear you in His gentle arms right now.

"The righteous cry out, and the LORD hears, and delivers them out of all their troubles."

~ Psalm 34:17 ~

If you belong to Him, God will always listen when you call to Him for help.

"Bear one another's burdens, and so fulfill the law of Christ."

~ Galatians 6:2 ~

When God has lightened your burdens, He asks you to do the same for others.

FOR THE WEIGHT OF THE WORLD

"When you pass through the waters,
I will be with you; and through the
rivers, they shall not overflow you.
... Fear not, for I am with you"

~ Isaiah 43:2, 5 ~

*Through faith His strength becomes yours,
and He reaches out to keep you from falling.*

. . . .

*Why not come to Jesus today and allow
Him to relieve you of your heavy load?*

BIBLE PROMISES FOR
WHEN YOU ARE
Feeling lonely

Are you feeling lonely? It's strange that, at times, one can be surrounded by people and still feel very alone. You can feel lonely even among people who love you; they may not understand what you're going through, at least not fully. But there is Someone who understands your heart completely. He knows your thoughts, feels your every emotion, and longs for you to know He's with you and for you. Take comfort in His promises ...

"And I will pray the Father, and He will give you another Helper, that He may abide with you forever— the Spirit of truth. ... I will not leave you orphans; I will come to you."

~ John 14:16–18 ~

You never need to feel abandoned because Jesus promised to be right there with you; He will even be, through His Holy Spirit, in you.

"God is our refuge and strength, a very present help in trouble."

~ Psalm 46:1 ~

So many troubling situations in life can leave you feeling alone and insecure, but God is a "very present help" at all times.

"When my father and my mother forsake me, then the LORD will take care of me."

~ Psalm 27:10 ~

Even when those closest to your heart turn away, the God of love will remain with you, safeguard you, and tenderly look after your needs.

"I am with you always, even to the end of the age."

~ Matthew 28:20 ~

As long as you desire His presence, there will never come a time when God will leave you to fend for yourself.

**"He heals the brokenhearted
and binds up their wounds."**

~ Psalm 147:3 ~

*Sometimes it's a broken heart that leaves
you feeling lonely, but the Lord promises to
heal the wounds and hold you close to Him.*

**"'For the mountains shall depart
and the hills be removed, but My
kindness shall not depart from you,
nor shall My covenant of peace
be removed,' says the LORD."**

~ Isaiah 54:10 ~

*God is so faithful that you can depend
on His care and attention even if the
mountains crumble around you!*

"In my distress I called upon the LORD,
and cried out to my God; He heard
my voice from His temple, and my cry
came before Him, even to His ears."

~ Psalm 18:6 ~

*You never have to feel that no one hears
you, because your heavenly Father
always hears and understands.*

"For I, the LORD your God, will
hold your right hand, saying to
you, 'Fear not, I will help you.'"

~ Isaiah 41:13 ~

*Loneliness will vanish when you realize
the Almighty God is holding your hand!*

"Be strong and of good courage ...
for the L ORD your God, He is the
One who goes with you. He will
not leave you nor forsake you."

~ Deuteronomy 31:6 ~

*The Creator of the universe is on your
team, and He will never leave you!*

. . . .

*Be encouraged in the loving presence
of your Savior, knowing He will always
stand beside you. And why not share
these verses with someone you love?*

BIBLE PROMISES FOR
WHEN YOU'VE HIT
Rock Bottom

So many circumstances in life can leave us feeling discouraged and helpless. But there's good reason to be optimistic; there's One who cares deeply about you. Read His promises …

"Call upon Me in the day of
trouble; I will deliver you, and
you shall glorify Me."

~ Psalm 50:15 ~

*The Lord is unlimited in His ability
to rescue you from any problem.*

"Why are you cast down, O my soul?
And why are you disquieted within
me? Hope in God, for I shall yet praise
Him for the help of His countenance."

~ Psalm 42:5 ~

*Your heavenly Father is the source of
all hope and is eager to help you.*

"He shall cover you with His feathers, and under His wings you shall take refuge; His truth shall be your shield and buckler."

~ Psalm 91:4 ~

In drawing close to God and seeking truth from His Word, you will find comfort and protection.

"You are my strong refuge."

~ Psalm 71:7 ~

You never need to feel alone with the all-powerful God of the universe by your side.

"For He will deliver the needy
when he cries, the poor also,
and him who has no helper."

~ Psalm 72:12 ~

*God is the Helper of the helpless and
loves to rescue those who call on Him.*

"From the end of the earth I will
cry to You, when my heart is
overwhelmed; lead me to the
rock that is higher than I."

~ Psalm 61:2 ~

*Ask God for help, and He will guide
you to an immovable foundation.*

"Trust in the LORD with all your
heart, and lean not on your
own understanding; in all your
ways acknowledge Him, and
He shall direct your paths."

~ Proverbs 3:5, 6 ~

*Lean totally on Him, look to Him
for guidance, and He will show
you what you need to do next.*

"For consider Him who endured such
hostility from sinners against Himself,
lest you become weary and discouraged
in your souls. You have not yet resisted
to bloodshed, striving against sin."

~ Hebrews 12:3, 4 ~

*The One who purposefully shed
His blood for you understands
what you are going through.*

"He also brought me up out of a horrible pit, out of the miry clay, and set my feet upon a rock, and established my steps."

~ Psalm 40:2 ~

As dreadful as your circumstances may appear, God has a perfect plan to get you back on solid ground.

"I am with you always, even to the end of the age."

~ Matthew 28:20 ~

Jesus promises to accompany you through every circumstance of life.

**"He who has begun a good work
in you will complete it until
the day of Jesus Christ."**

~ Philippians 1:6 ~

*God fully intends to save you in His kingdom
of love; He isn't going to give up on you!*

. . . .

*Cry out to the Lord, trust in Him, lean
on Him, seek Him with all your being,
wait patiently on Him, and He will help
you conquer every difficulty you face!*

BIBLE PROMISES FOR
WHEN YOU ARE FEELING
Stressed

Nearly everyone experiences some level of stress on a daily basis, and sometimes it can get out of hand. Thankfully, God's Word gives helpful direction on how to find relief for whatever is pressuring you ...

"I have set the LORD always before me; because He is at my right hand I shall not be moved."

~ Psalm 16:8 ~

Know first that God is with you at all times and is watching over you.

"Be still, and know that I am God."

~ Psalm 46:10 ~

Do you ever find the frantic rush of life eclipsing your focus on God and His Word? It's critical to take time for quietness with Him.

"Be anxious for nothing, but in everything by prayer and supplication, with thanksgiving, let your requests be made known to God; and the peace of God, which surpasses all understanding, will guard your hearts and minds through Christ Jesus."

~ Philippians 4:6, 7 ~

After you've listened for His still small voice, tell your heavenly Father exactly what you need, and receive His immeasurable peace.

"Take My yoke upon you and learn from Me, for I am gentle and lowly in heart, and you will find rest for your souls."

~ Matthew 11:29 ~

If you seek Christ and live in obedience to Him, He will give you calming rest.

"You will keep him in perfect peace, whose mind is stayed on You, because he trusts in You."

~ Isaiah 26:3 ~

Focusing on God and trusting in Him results in His perfect peace expanding in your heart.

"Better a handful with quietness than both hands full, together with toil and grasping for the wind."

~ Ecclesiastes 4:6 ~

Being thankful and content with what you have is another key to beating stress.

"Remember the Sabbath day, to keep it holy."

~ Exodus 20:8 ~

Observing the weekly seventh-day Sabbath and keeping it holy is one of the greatest blessings and de-stressors God has given to mankind!

"My brethren, count it all joy when you fall into various trials, knowing that the testing of your faith produces patience. But let patience have its perfect work, that you may be perfect and complete, lacking nothing."

~ James 1:2–4 ~

If you find yourself in the midst of trouble, be patient and remember that God has the power to bring good things even from your trials.

"Then He arose and rebuked the wind, and said to the sea, 'Peace, be still!' And the wind ceased and there was a great calm."

~ Mark 4:39 ~

Just as Jesus quieted the storm at sea, He will gladly quiet your anxious thoughts and soothe your troubled mind!

"And He said to them, 'Come aside by yourselves to a deserted place and rest a while.' For there were many coming and going, and they did not even have time to eat."

~ Mark 6:31 ~

As Jesus' disciple, you need regular times of re-creation and rest to maintain good physical and emotional health.

. . . .

Why not ask your loving Savior right now to carry your burdens and quiet you with His infinite love?

BIBLE PROMISES FOR WHEN YOU FEEL

Tempted

Temptation happens regularly to all of us. Remember, there's nothing wrong in being tempted. After all, even Jesus was tempted, but of course He overcame each temptation. It's only when we give in to the temptation that we fail, but that never needs to happen. Read on and hold tight to His promises …

"For in that He Himself has suffered, being tempted, He is able to aid those who are tempted."

~ Hebrews 2:18 ~

Jesus understands from experience what you are facing and will help you get through it victoriously if you trust in Him.

"You are of God, little children, and have overcome them, because He who is in you is greater than he who is in the world."

~ 1 John 4:4 ~

It's not your strength that matters, but the strength of Christ in you!

"No temptation has overtaken you except such as is common to man; but God is faithful, who will not allow you to be tempted beyond what you are able, but with the temptation will also make the way of escape."

~ 1 Corinthians 10:13 ~

You may think you suffer alone in a particular temptation, but you can be sure others have been there; with God's help you'll find a way out!

"Therefore let him who thinks he stands take heed lest he fall."

~ 1 Corinthians 10:12 ~

When things are going smoothly, it's easy to fall into a pattern of putting trust in yourself; that's when you're most vulnerable to temptation.

"Therefore submit to God. Resist
the devil and he will flee from
you. Draw near to God and He
will draw near to you."

~ James 4:7,8 ~

*Your part in overcoming temptation is to
resist it and to seek God with all your heart!*

"Your word I have hidden in my heart,
that I might not sin against You."

~ Psalm 119:11 ~

*Fill your mind with Scripture and
those verses will return to support you
just when you need them most; this
is how Jesus defeated temptation!*

"Be strong in the Lord and in the power of His might. Put on the whole armor of God, that you may be able to stand against the wiles of the devil."

~ Ephesians 6:10, 11 ~

You can never stand against the enemy in your own strength, but Jesus offers you His strength to resist temptation.

"Now to Him who is able to keep you from stumbling, and to present you faultless before the presence of His glory with exceeding joy."

~ Jude 1:24 ~

God won't give up on you; He wants you with Him forever!

"These things I write to you, so that you may not sin. And if anyone sins, we have an Advocate with the Father, Jesus Christ the righteous."

~ 1 John 2:1 ~

If you fall, don't be discouraged; God promises you forgiveness and a fresh start through Jesus Christ!

. . . .

The One who overcame all temptation to win eternal life for you, also promises He will be with you each day and give you the strength to win every battle!

BIBLE PROMISES for
WHEN YOU FEEL THAT

No One Cares

The world can be such an uncaring
place, and circumstances can leave
you feeling cold, empty, and alone.
Sometimes it's easy to forget that God
loves you personally and deeply and
cares very much about your welfare.
Look at His uplifting words for you …

"For I know the thoughts that I
think toward you, says the LORD,
thoughts of peace and not of evil,
to give you a future and a hope."

~ Jeremiah 29:11 ~

*Whatever your situation right
now, God is for you and has
wonderful plans for your life.*

"The one who comes to Me I
will by no means cast out."

~ John 6:37 ~

*Regardless of your past, the arms of the
Savior are outstretched to you in welcome.*

"The eternal God is your refuge, and underneath are the everlasting arms."

~ Deuteronomy 33:27 ~

The Lord will shelter you from the harshness of this world, supporting you with His arms of love.

"The LORD is near to those who have a broken heart, and saves such as have a contrite spirit."

~ Psalm 34:18 ~

If your heart is broken today, be assured that God understands and is right there with you, desiring to heal your wounded spirit.

"Blessed be the God and Father of our Lord Jesus Christ, the Father of mercies and God of all comfort, who comforts us in all our tribulation."

~ 2 Corinthians 1:3, 4 ~

His mercy toward you is unfathomable, and He is always ready to comfort you in whatever you are experiencing.

**"Casting all your care upon
Him, for He cares for you."**

~ 1 Peter 5:7 ~

*God doesn't turn away when you unload
your burdens on Him; even if all your
friends and family were to abandon
you, God would still care for you.*

**"I have loved you with an
everlasting love; therefore with
lovingkindness I have drawn you."**

~ Jeremiah 31:3 ~

*God's love for you is limitless;
He loves you forever!*

"For He Himself has said, 'I will never leave you nor forsake you.'"

~ Hebrews 13:5 ~

Jesus, who died to save you, is more faithful than any earthly friend, and He promised to stay beside you always.

"Behold what manner of love the Father has bestowed on us, that we should be called children of God!"

~ 1 John 3:1 ~

When you come to God, you become part of His family of love and God accepts you as His own child!

"He shall cover you with His feathers, and under His wings you shall take refuge; His truth shall be your shield and buckler."

~ Psalm 91:4 ~

If you seek God and trust in Him, He will defend you just as a protective eagle parent that spreads its wings over its chicks.

. . . .

Whatever you are facing today, know that God's heart overflows with love and concern for you and that He will stay with you and help you through any difficulty.

WHEN YOU NEED
BIBLE TRUTH

Bible knowledge brings peace, hope, and happiness. That's why we invite you to explore these incredible websites full of trustworthy information about the Bible—you will be wowed and blessed with every click!

....

TruthAboutDeath.com

What really happens when we die? Explore what the Bible really has to say—you'll be amazed and blessed and encouraged with the truth!

SabbathTruth.com

God has designed a special day for all mankind. What happened to that day? How can you receive the promises of it today? The truth is just around the corner!

HellTruth.com

What the Bible really says about hellfire will amaze you and bring you peace and comfort. A true understanding about hell will transform your understanding of God.

GhostTruth.com

What does the Bible say about ghosts? The Bible truth is so important that you simply don't want to miss visiting this website!

666Truth.com

A lot of misinformation about the mark of the beast is circulating through the Christian church! Get a Bible-based perspective that actually makes sense!

BibleProphecyTruth.com

Do you want to better understand Bible prophecy and how it affects you? Then don't wait to visit this vast website full of prophecy information you can trust!

Explore the Bible in-depth at these sites ...

AmazingFacts.org
BibleHistory.com
BibleUniverse.com
ProphecySeminars.com

Follow us on Facebook, Twitter, and YouTube!

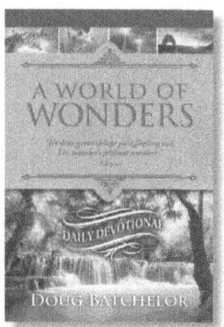

A World of Wonders
A Daily Devotional

Enjoy Pastor Doug's first-ever daily devotional! Drawing from history, nature, science, and technology, these 366 devotionals provide fascinating facts and powerful spiritual messages. Teens and kids will love the concise and interesting entries!

AF-WGDD ... $19.95

NKJV Prophecy Study Bibles

These brilliant study Bibles from Amazing Facts combine the easy-to-understand language and accuracy of the New King James Version with a special emphasis on prophecy to supercharge your spiritual life! Loaded with helpful features: all 27 Amazing Facts Study Guides, The Biblical Cyclopedic Index, 64-page Concordance, Words of Christ in Red, Doug Batchelor's "Studying the Bible," and much more!

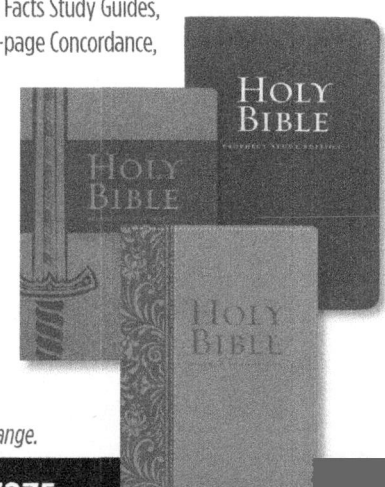

Giant Print Premium Leather
BK-PSBGPL ... $99.95

Navy Blue Leathersoft (Sword)
BK-PSBNL ... $76.95

Teal Leathersoft (Floral Pattern)
BK-PSBTL ... $76.95

Prices subject to change.

or call **800-538-7275**